TAKEN TO HEART

Taken to Heart

70 Poems from the Chinese

Translated by Gary Young & Yanwen Xu

WHITE PINE PRESS | BUFFALO, NEW YORK

Publication of this book was supported by public funds from the New York State Council on the Arts, with the support of Governor Kathy Hochul and the New York State Legislature, a State Agency; with funds from The Amazon Literary Partnership; and by a Miramar Editions Jon Veinberg Memorial Grant.

Cover art: 'Nanzhi' (Early Spring) by Wang Mian, 1287-1359.

Title page: Rubbing of calligraphic stele by Su Shi, 1036-1101.

Book design by Gary Young.

Cover design by Elaine LaMattina.

Acknowledgments can be found on page 97.

Printed and bound in the United States of America.

First Edition

ISBN:978-1-945680-58-8

Library of Congress Control Number: 2022930228

White Pine Press
P. O. Box 236
Buffalo, NY 14201

www.whitepine.org

for Dennis Maloney

CONTENTS

Introduction | *xi*

POEMS

INTRODUCTION

THE SEVENTY POEMS that comprise this collection constitute an anthology, "Elementary School Chinese Textbook (Jiangsu Edition)", given to Chinese school children as a text to aid their instruction in Mandarin, and to introduce them to China's rich literary history. The poems are considered representative of China's highest poetic achievements from the Han Dynasty to the Qing. The study of these poems is also meant to subtly guide students toward an appreciation of traditional Chinese virtues, culture, historical events, and social etiquette. The poems are memorized by every student, and by the end of their course of study, Chinese children will have absorbed a storehouse of Chinese characters and been steeped in a cultural tradition that spans more than two thousand years.

We have striven to mirror the emotional state and the musical values of the originals. We chose to translate primarily line by line, and have eschewed jumbling lines within individual poems. Chinese is such an allusive language, we could never hope to achieve the same concision in English, but we have tried to ring the appropriate notes, and to privilege characters with the closest English equivalents. Our primary motive has been to create moving poems in American English that capture as much of the original Chinese in mood, texture, and spirit as possible.

GY
YX

TAKEN TO HEART

FOLK RHYME (Han Dynasty)

South of the Yangtze River

Let's go to Jiangnan and pick lotus!
The blossoms are beautiful,
And fish play among the lotus leaves.
The fish play among the lotus leaves to the east,
The fish play among the lotus leaves to the west,
The fish play among the lotus leaves to the south,
The fish play among the lotus leaves to the north.

江南

北朝民歌（南北朝）

江南可采莲，
莲叶何田田！
鱼戏莲叶间。
鱼戏莲叶东，
鱼戏莲叶西。
鱼戏莲叶南，
鱼戏莲叶北。

Song of Chi Le

The Chi Le Plain
Spreads out from
The dark foot of Mt. Yin.
The ashen sky is like a yurt,
A dome over the vast expanse
Where wind moves the grass
Around oxen and sheep.

敕勒歌

北朝民歌（南北朝）

敕勒川，
阴山下，
天似穹庐，
笼盖四野。
天苍苍，
野茫茫，
风吹草低见牛羊。

LUO BINWANG (Tang)

An Ode to the Geese

Geese, geese, geese—
Bend their necks and sing to the sky.
White feathers float on green water,
And red webbed feet churn up ripples.

咏鹅

骆宾王（唐）

鹅, 鹅, 鹅,
曲项向天歌。
白毛浮绿水,
红掌拨清波。

LI QIAO (Tang)

Wind

Slashes the leaves in autumn,
And wakes the blossoms in spring.
On the river, it raises thousand-foot waves,
And in the bamboo forest, a million poles are bent.

风

李峤 （唐）

解落三秋叶，
能开二月花。
过江千尺浪，
入竹万竿斜。

HE ZHIZHANG (Tang)

An Ode to the Willows

Jade has disguised itself as a willow
Hung with a thousand ribbons of green silk.
No one knows who tailored the slender leaves,
But the spring breeze cuts like a blade.

咏柳

贺知章 （唐）

碧玉妆成一树高，
万条垂下绿丝绦。
不知细叶谁裁出，
二月春风似剪刀。

WANG ZHIHUAN (Tang)

A Song of Liangzhou

The Yellow River flows from the clouds
Past mountains and lonely towns.
Don't play that sad song, don't break a willow branch,
The spring breeze will never reach us here at the border.

凉州词

王之涣 （唐）

黄河远上白云间，
一片孤城万仞山。
羌笛何须怨杨柳，
春风不度玉门关。

WANG ZHIHUAN (Tang)

Climbing White Stork Tower

The white sun disappears behind the mountains,
And the Yellow River flows into the sea.
You can take in the whole horizon
If you climb up one more story.

登鹳雀楼

王之焕 （唐）

白日依山尽，
黄河入海流。
欲穷千里目，
更上一层楼。

MENG HAORAN (Tang)

Spring Morning

It's easy to sleep past dawn in spring
When trilling birds can be heard from every direction.
All last night, there was the cry of wind and rain.
Who can know how many flowers lay in ruins?

春晓

孟浩然 （唐）

春眠不觉晓，
处处闻啼鸟。
夜来风雨声，
花落知多少。

WANG HAN (Tang)

The Song of Liangzhou

I want to keep drinking wine from this luminous cup,
But someone on horseback has blown the battle call.
Don't laugh if I fall drunk on the killing field.
Even in ancient times, how many ever made it back?

凉州词

王翰 （唐）

葡萄美酒夜光杯，
欲饮琵琶马上催。
醉卧沙场君莫笑，
古来征战几人回？

WANG CHANGLING (Tang)

Crossing the Border

A bright moon shines on the border that never changes.
The soldiers sent on foreign campaigns have yet to return.
If only we still had General Li, or General Wei,
These barbarians would never get past the Yin Mountains!

出塞

王昌龄 （唐）

秦时明月汉时关，
万里长征人未还。
但使龙城飞将在，
不教胡马度阴山！

WANG CHANGLING (Tang)

Bidding Farewell to Jian Xin Beside the Hibiscus Tower

Last night we floated downriver in a cold rain.
In the morning, when my friend leaves, I'll be left alone
   with the mountains.
If anyone asks how I'm doing,
Tell them my heart is like clear ice in a bowl of pure jade.

芙蓉楼送辛渐

王昌龄 (唐)

寒雨连江夜入吴，
平明送客楚山孤。
洛阳亲友如相问，
一片冰心在玉壶。

WANG WEI (Tang)

Deer Park

The mountains are empty, no one around,
But from somewhere, the sound of voices.
Deep in the forest
Light glints off green moss.

鹿柴
王维 （唐）

空山不见人，
但闻人语响。
返景入深林，
复照青苔上。

WANG WEI (Tang)

Farewell to Yuan'er Departing for Anxi

Morning rain washes the dust from Weicheng.
The willows and the guest house are now the same vivid green.
Have one more cup of wine,
You'll find no friends on the other side of the border.

送元二使安西

王维 （唐）

渭城朝雨浥轻尘，
客舍青青柳色新。
劝君更尽一杯酒，
西出阳关无故人。

WANG WEI (Tang)

On the Double Nine Festival, I Think about My Brothers

Far from home, alone in a foreign town,
The festival arrives, and I miss my family more than ever.
I know that everyone will have climbed the hill
    outside our village
And put their hair up with a sprig of dogwood,
    but one of us is missing.

九月九日忆山东兄弟

王维 （唐）

独在异乡为异客，
每逢佳节倍思亲。
遥知兄弟登高处，
遍插茱萸少一人。

LI BAI (Tang)

Night Thoughts

The bright moonlight on my bed
Looks like frost across the bedroom floor.
I lift my head to look at the moon,
And when I lie back down, I think of home.

静夜思

李白（唐）

床前明月光，
疑是地上霜。
举头望明月，
低头思故乡。

LI BAI (Tang)

Walking in Moonlight (excerpt)

When I was young, I didn't understand the moon.
I thought it was a white plate made of jade,
Or a mirror from heaven
That had flown to the top of the clouds.

古朗月行 (节录)

李白 (唐)

小时不识月，
呼作白玉盘。
又疑瑶台镜，
飞在青云端。

LI BAI (Tang)

Gazing at Lu Shan Waterfall

Smoke from incense turns blue in sunlight.
The waterfall below hangs like cloth
Flowing so far down the mountain
It could be the Milky Way fallen from the sky.

望庐山瀑布

李白 （唐）

日照香炉生紫烟，
遥看瀑布挂前川。
飞流直下三千尺，
疑是银河落九天。

LI BAI (Tang)

For Wang Lun

While boarding a boat to leave,
I hear someone playing music on the riverbank.
The waters of Peach Blossom Lake are a thousand feet deep,
But not as deep as my love for Wang Lun.

赠汪伦

李白（唐）

李白乘舟将欲行，
忽闻岸上踏歌声。
桃花潭水深千尺，
不及汪伦送我情。

LI BAI (Tang)

Farewell from Yellow Crane Tower to Meng Haoran Who Is Leaving for Yangzhou

My old friend is leaving Yellow Crane Tower for the East.
He sails through fog and spring blossoms
    on his way to Yangzhou,
And I watch until his boat disappears
Where the Yangtze River meets the sky.

黄鹤楼送孟浩然之广陵

李白 （唐）

故人西辞黄鹤楼，
烟花三月下扬州。
孤帆远影碧空尽，
唯见长江天际流。

LI BAI (Tang)

Departing Baidi City in Early Morning

I leave Baidi City early in the morning under colorful clouds.
Jiangling may be a thousand miles away, but I'll get back
   in a single day.
Monkeys howl on the riverbanks,
And already, my swift, light boat has passed a thousand peaks.

早发白帝城

李白 （唐）

朝辞白帝彩云间，
千里江陵一日还。
两岸猿声啼不住，
轻舟已过万重山。

Gazing at Tianmen Mountain

The River Chu splits the Tianmen Mountains at Heaven's Gate.
The water flows east, then west as it loops around the gorge.
Green mountains rise and face one another
    on either side of the river.
A single boat sails before the setting sun.

望天门山

李白（唐）

天门中断楚江开，
碧水东流至此回。
两岸青山相对出，
孤帆一片日边来。

GAO SHI (Tang)

Farewell to Dong Tinglan

The sun is hazy, barely visible behind endless yellow clouds.
A cold north wind carries wild geese away, and the snow
   falls and falls.
Don't worry about making friends,
Who in the world wouldn't recognize you?

别董大

高适（唐）

千里黄云白日曛，
北风吹雁雪纷纷。
莫愁前路无知己，
天下谁人不识君？

DU FU (Tang)

Quatrain (1)

Two Orioles sing on an emerald-green willow.
A line of egrets flies across the clear blue sky.
Framed by the window, years of snow on the western ridge.
The boats docked at the door have traveled a thousand miles
    from Dong Wu.

绝句
杜甫（唐）

两个黄鹂鸣翠柳，
一行白鹭上青天。
窗含西岭千秋雪，
门泊东吴万里船。

DU FU (Tang)

A Pleasing Rain on a Spring Night

The spring rain came last night
As if it knew when to arrive,
Sneaking in with the wind to dampen
And nourish everything without a sound.
The trails now are dark under the black clouds,
But sparks rise from boats on the river.
This morning, the flowers and plants
Are all bent in Jin'guan City.

春夜喜雨

杜甫（唐）

好雨知时节，
当春乃发生。
随风潜入夜，
润物细无声。
野径云俱黑，
江船火独明。
晓看红湿处，
花重锦官城。

Quatrain (2)

The countryside is lovely in late spring.
The scent of fragrant blossoms drifts on the breeze.
Swallows gather mud to build their nests,
And ducks sleep side-by-side on the warm sand.

绝句

杜甫（唐）

迟日江山丽，
春风花草香。
泥融飞燕子，
沙暖睡鸳鸯。

DU FU (Tang)

Walking Alone by the Riverbank Looking for Flowers

The river flows east past a yellow tower,
And I'm soothed by a cool, lazy breeze.
This cluster of peach blossoms belongs to no one.
I cannot say which I love more, the pink ones, or the red.

江畔独步寻花

杜甫（唐）

黄师塔前江水东，
春光懒困倚微风。
桃花一簇开无主，
可爱深红爱浅红？

ZHANG JI (Tang)

Docked by Maple Bridge at Night

Crows cry out as the moon sinks through frosty air.
Light from a fishing boat shines on Maple Bridge,
    and sleep will not come.
Outside Gusu City, the midnight bells ringing in Hanshan Temple
Can be heard from the passing boats.

枫桥夜泊

张继（唐）

月落乌啼霜满天，
江枫渔火对愁眠。
姑苏城外寒山寺，
夜半钟声到客船。

MENG JIAO (Tang)

Traveler's Lament

A loving mother sews
Traveling clothes for her son.
She wonders when he'll return,
And with each stitch, her knots get tighter.
Her son knows the spring grass
Owes a debt to the sunlight it cannot repay.

游子吟

孟郊（唐）

慈母手中线，
游子身上衣。
临行密密缝，
意恐迟迟归。
谁言寸草心，
报得三春晖。

Snow on the River

Birds have fled the mountains,
And people have left no trace.
An old man in a raincoat and a broad hat
Fishes the cold river.

江雪

柳宗元（唐）

千山鸟飞绝，
万径人踪灭。
孤舟蓑笠翁，
独钓寒江雪。

ZHANG ZHIHE (Tang)

Fisherman's Song

White egrets fly before the Xisai Mountains.
Peach blossoms float on the river above a school of fat perch.
In a green bamboo hat, and a raincoat made of dark grass,
A fisherman turns into the wind—a little rain doesn't bother him.

渔歌子

张志和（唐）

西塞山前白鹭飞，
桃花流水鳜鱼肥。
青箬笠，绿蓑衣，
斜风细雨不须归。

Border Song

Geese flew off in the dim moonlight
While Chan Yu made his escape.
Soldiers rode after him
With snow on their bows and blades.

塞下曲

卢纶（唐）

月黑雁飞高，
单于夜遁逃。
欲将轻骑逐，
大雪满弓刀。

LIU YUXI (Tang)

Gazing at Dongting Lake

The surface of the lake harmonizes with autumn moonlight
And becomes a fogged mirror of bronze.
A hill rises from the center of Dongting Lake
Like a small green snail on a silver plate.

望洞庭

刘禹锡（唐）

湖光秋月两相和，
潭面无风镜未磨。
遥望洞庭山水翠，
白银盘里一青螺。

LIU YUXI (Tang)

Waves of Sand

The Yellow River runs heavy with sand for a thousand miles,
Waves churning in a wind that blows from the edge of heaven.
The river flows straight to the Milky Way
Where two lovers meet, but only for a day.

浪淘沙

刘禹锡（唐）

九曲黄河万里沙，
浪淘风簸自天涯。
如今直上银河去，
同到牵牛织女家。

BAI JUYI (Tang)

In Response to an Exam Question, I Write about 'Farewells on Ancient Ground'

Dense grass grows
Through the year, then withers.
Wildfires may burn it out,
But spring breezes breathe life back into it.
Emerald weeds overgrow
The old road connecting abandoned towns.
Friends bid farewell,
And even the lush grass seems sad.

赋得古原草送别

白居易（唐）

离离原上草，
一岁一枯荣。
野火烧不尽，
春风吹又生。
远芳侵古道，
晴翠接荒城。
又送王孙去，
萋萋满别情。

BAI JUYI (Tang)

On the Pond

A child steers his tiny boat back to shore
After stealing a white lotus.
He doesn't realize
That he's left a trail through the duckweed.

池上

白居易 （唐）

小娃撑小艇，
偷采白莲回。
不解藏踪迹，
浮萍一道开。

BAI JUYI (Tang)

Remembering Jiangnan

Jiangnan is just as lovely as I remember.
At sunrise, the lapping river glows red as fire,
And in springtime, the water turns from green to glassy blue.
Who could ever forget Jiangnan?

忆江南

白居易（唐）

江南好，风景旧曾谙。
日出江花红胜火，
春来江水绿如蓝。
能不忆江南？

HU LINGNENG (Tang)

Small Child Fishing

A child with hair cut like a lotus is trying to fish
From a mossy bank, his body half-hidden in the grass.
He waves away travelers who ask him questions,
And afraid of scaring the fish, ignores them.

小儿垂钓

胡令能 （唐）

蓬头稚子学垂纶，
侧坐莓苔草映身。
路人借问遥招手，
怕得鱼惊不应人。

LI SHEN (Tang)

Turning the Soil

The soil is turned in the heat of the day,
And sweat drips into the ground.
Every grain of rice in your bowl
Is born out of suffering.

锄禾

李绅（唐）

锄禾日当午，
汗滴禾下土。
谁知盘中餐，
粒粒皆辛苦。

LI SHEN (Tang)

Pity the Farmer

You plant one seed in the spring,
And harvest a thousand seeds in autumn.
No farmland is left untilled,
But farmers still starve to death.

悯农

李绅（唐）

春种一粒粟，
秋收万颗子。
四海无闲田，
农夫犹饿死。

JIA DAO (Tang)

Seeking the Hidden One

I ask a boy under a pine tree about my friend,
And he says, my teacher is away picking herbs.
I only know he's in the mountains,
Somewhere inside the thick clouds.

寻隐者不遇
贾岛（唐）

松下问童子，
言师采药去。
只在此山中，
云深不知处。

DU MU (Tang)

Traveling Through the Mountains

Climbing a cold, stone path in the mountains,
Houses can be seen faintly through the clouds.
Late in the evening, I stop my cart to look at the maples,
More brilliant than any flower in spring.

山行

杜牧（唐）

远上寒山石径斜，
白云深处有人家。
停车坐爱枫林晚，
霜叶红于二月花。

DU MU (Tang)

Qingming

It always seems to rain during the Qingming Festival,
When people walk as if their souls had wandered away.
Do you know where I can get a drink?
A shepherd boy points to Apricot Blossom Village,
    far in the distance.

清明

杜牧（唐）

清明时节雨纷纷，
路上行人欲断魂。
借问酒家何处有，
牧童遥指杏花村。

DU MU (Tang)

Spring in Jiangnan

A thousand warblers call out among the flowers and trees.
Below the mountains, wine flags wave in a village on the water.
Five hundred temples were built in the south,
And they all fell to ruin in the fog and rain.

江南春

杜（唐）

千里莺啼绿映红，
水村山郭酒旗风。
南朝四百八十寺，
多少楼台烟雨中。

LI SHANGYIN (Tang)

Happiness on Le You Heights

Downhearted at nightfall,
I leave my cart and climb to Le You.
The setting sun is so beautiful,
But too soon, it will be dark.

乐游原

李商隐（唐）

向晚意不适，
驱车登古原。
夕阳无限好，
只是近黄昏。

Bee

Whether on the flatlands or in the mountains,
The bees are there.
They collect honey from a hundred flowers,
But who are they working for?

蜂

罗隐（唐）

不论平地与山尖，
无限风光尽被占。
采得百花成蜜后，
为谁辛苦为谁甜？

FAN ZHONGYAN (Song)

Fishermen on the River

Travelers on the river
Love the taste of perch.
The fisherman's boat, small as a leaf,
Fights the wind and waves.

江上渔者

范仲淹（宋）

江上往来人，
但爱鲈鱼美。
君看一叶舟，
出没风波里。

WANG ANSHI (Song)

New Year's Day

The old year dies with the sound of firecrackers.
Spring brings a warm breeze, and everyone drinks *toso* wine.
Each house is bathed in morning light,
And the neighbors change out their old peach boards for new.

元日

王安石（宋）

爆竹声中一岁除，
春风送暖入屠苏。
千门万户瞳瞳日，
总把新桃换旧符。

WANG ANSHI (Song)

Docking at Guazhou

This river runs from Jingkou to Guazhou,
And Zhongshan lies just beyond the mountains.
The wind has carried spring to the southern bank of the river.
How long before the moon lights my way back home?

泊船瓜洲

王安石（宋）

京口瓜洲一水间，
钟山只隔数重山。
春风又绿江南岸，
明月何时照我还。

WANG ANSHI (Song)

Written on Mr. Lake's Wall

Mr. Lake sweeps the moss from his courtyard
Surrounded by trees and flowers he's planted himself.
A winding stream wraps around his fields and keeps them green.
He opens his door to the distant, blue-green mountains.

书湖阴先生壁

王安石（宋）

茅檐长扫净无苔，
花木成畦手自栽。

SU SHI (Song)

June 27, I Write a Poem While Drunk in Wanghu Tower

Ink-dark clouds cover everything below the mountains.
Raindrops like white pearls bounce onto the boats below.
Suddenly a strong wind blows everything away,
And the water beneath the tower is as clear as the sky.

六月二十七日望湖楼醉书

苏轼（宋）

黑云翻墨未遮山，
白雨跳珠乱入船。
卷地风来忽吹散，
望湖楼下水如天。

SU SHI (Song)

Drinking on West Lake
After Rain Disturbs a Clear Sky

Sunlight shimmers on the ripples under a dazzling clear sky.
The mountains, masked by fog and misty showers,
   are otherworldly.
West Lake is as lovely as the most beautiful woman,
Lightly powdered or heavily rouged, she always looks perfect.

饮湖上初晴后雨

苏轼（宋）

水光潋艳晴方好，
山色空朦雨欲奇。
欲把西湖比西子，
淡妆浓抹总相宜。

SU SHI (Song)

A River in Spring for Hui Chong

Peach trees bloom beside a stand of bamboo.
Ducks are the first to know when the river warms.
Tender shoots of reeds and mugwort line the bank.
Now is the time to hunt river dolphin.

惠崇春江晚景

苏轼（宋）

竹外桃花三两枝，
春江水暖鸭先知。
蒌蒿满地芦芽短，
正是河豚欲上时。

SU SHI (Song)

Written on the Wall
of Xi Lin Temple

Across the horizon, it looks like a ridge,
    but from the side, a peak.
Whether I'm near or far, high or low, it always looks different.
I can't recognize the true face of Mt. Lu
Because I am inside the mountain.

题西林壁

苏轼（宋）

横看成岭侧成峰，
远近高低各不同。
不识庐山真面目，
只缘身在此山中。

LI QINGZHAO (Song)

A Four-Line Poem Composed in Summer

Alive, be a hero among the living,
Dead, be a hero among the dead.
I still miss Xiangyu,
Who refused to retreat across the river.

夏日绝句

李清照（宋）

生当作人杰，
死亦为鬼雄。
至今思项羽，
不肯过江东。

LU YOU (Song)

To My Son

When I die, all I see now will vanish,
And I'm sorry that I won't live to see the country reunited.
When the government in exile returns from the south,
Don't forget to bring me the news when you visit my grave.

示儿

陆游（宋）

死去元知万事空，
但悲不见九州同。
王师北定中原日，
家祭无忘告乃翁。

LU YOU (Song)

I Walk Through My Gate Before Dawn to Feel the Cool Air

The Yellow River still flows to the eastern sea,
And Mt. Hua still reaches to the sky.
Covered by the dust of the invaders,
Year after year, we wait for the Emperor's army to return.

秋夜将晓出篱门迎凉有感

陆游（宋）

三万里河东入海，
五千仞岳上摩天。
遗民泪尽胡尘里，
南望王师又一年。

FAN CHENGDA (Song)

from 'Four Pastoral Poems'
(Summer) 1

Farmers enter their fields at dawn, and at dusk,
　　return home and spin thread.
In the village, the older children tend to the houses.
The youngest children are too small to plow or to weave,
In the shade of a mulberry, they pretend to plant melons.

四时田园杂兴

范成大（宋）

昼出耘田夜绩麻，
村庄儿女各当家。
童孙未解供耕织，
也傍桑阴学种瓜。

FAN CHENGDA (SONG)

from 'Four Pastoral Poems' (Summer) 2

The apricots have turned golden, and the plums grow fat.
The buckwheat blossoms are white as snow,
   though the rapeseed is sparse.
It's been a long time since anyone's passed through this field.
There's no one here but dragonflies and butterflies darting about.

四时田园杂兴
范成大（宋）

梅子金黄杏子肥，
麦花雪白菜花稀。
日长篱落无人过，
唯有蜻蜓蛱蝶飞。

YANG WANLI (Song)

Little Pool

A tiny spring trickles just enough to fill a pond.
The shadow of a tree rests tenderly on the water.
A lotus bud has broken the surface,
And already, a dragonfly has landed there.

小池

杨万里（宋）

泉眼无声惜细流，
树阴照水爱晴柔。
小荷才露尖尖角，
早有蜻蜓立上头。

YANG WANLI (Song)

At Dawn I Leave Jingci Temple to Bid Farewell to Lin Zifang

West Lake in mid-June
Is more beautiful than at any other time.
Jade-green lotus leaves touch the sky,
And their blossoms, struck by sunlight, are impossibly red.

晓出净慈寺送林子方

杨万里（宋）

毕竟西湖六月中，
风光不与四时同。
接天莲叶无穷碧，
映日荷花别样红。

ZHU XI (Song)

Spring Day

On this bright spring morning beside the River Si,
    everything is glorious.
The world has been renewed, and there's no end
    to the beauty all around.
Even a fool could recognize this warm breeze
    as the face of spring,
And it would still be spring no matter the color of the flowers.

春日

朱熹（宋）

胜日寻芳泗水滨，
无边光景一时新。
等闲识得东风面，
万紫千红总是春。

LIN SHENG   (Song)

Writing on the Wall of an Inn in Lin'an

Green mountains all around, and so many buildings.
When will they ever stop singing and dancing around West Lake?
Everyone here is so drunk on the warm spring breeze,
They think they're in Bianzhou, the lost capital,
    not here in Hangzhou.

题临安邸

林升（宋）

山外青山楼外楼，
西湖歌舞几时休？
暖风熏得游人醉，
直把杭州做汴州。

YE SHAOWENG   (Song)

I Try to Enter a Garden, but I Can't Get In

Perhaps he's afraid my wooden shoes will damage his moss.
I knocked on the door, but the door never opened.
It's impossible to wall in the beauty of spring,
An apricot branch draped in red blossoms
    has crept over the wall.

游园不值

叶绍翁（宋）

应怜屐齿印苍苔，
小扣柴扉久不开。
春色满园关不住，
一枝红杏出墙来。

WENG JUAN (Song)

April in the Countryside

The mountains are green, the wetlands white
   with the reflection of the sky.
The cry of the cuckoos can be heard through the mist.
In April, there are few idle hands in the village.
Finished with silkworm and mulberry, it's time now to plant rice.

乡村四月
翁卷（宋）

绿遍山原白满川，
子规声里雨如烟。
乡村四月闲人少，
才了蚕桑又插田。

WANG MIAN   (Song)

Inky Plum

There's a plum tree beside the pool where I clean my inkstone,
And on each blossom there is a trace of ink.
It doesn't matter if anyone compliments the color,
Only that the pure scent of the blossom fills the world.

墨梅

王冕（宋）

我家洗砚池头树，
朵朵花开淡墨痕。
不要人夸颜色好，
只留清气满乾坤。

YU QIAN (Ming)

Limestone

Hammers and chisels bring the stone up
  from deep within the mountains.
The stone is baked by a raging fire, and feels nothing.
Its bones are crushed into powder, and it's not afraid,
It will remain in the world, clean, white, and innocent.

石灰吟
于谦（宋）

千锤万凿出深山，
烈火焚烧若等闲。
粉身碎骨浑不怕，
要留清白在人间。

ZHENG XIE (Qing)

Bamboo in the Rocks

It clings to the mountain, and won't let go,
The roots are buried deep inside the broken stones.
Blowing sand may grind it, and wind may batter and bend it,
But it doesn't care at all about the wind—
　　north, south, east, or west.

竹石
郑燮 （清）

咬定青山不放松，
立根原在破岩中。
千磨万击还坚韧，
任尔东西南北风。

YUAN MEI (Qing)

What I Saw

A shepherd boy riding a yellow cow,
His song echoing through the trees.
He wanted to catch a chirping cicada,
So shot up with a start, and stopped singing.

所见
袁枚（清）

牧童骑黄牛，
歌声振林樾。
意欲捕鸣蝉，
忽然闭口立。

GAO DING (Qing)

Living in the Country

The grass grows tall, and a warbler flies overhead. It's February,
The branches of the willow graze the riverbank, and I'm drunk
    on the misty haze.
The children have come home early from school
To try and catch the wind with their kites.

村居

高鼎（清）

草长莺飞二月天，
拂堤杨柳醉春烟。
儿童散学归来早，
忙趁东风放纸鸢。

GONG ZIZHEN (Qing)

from 'Miscellaneous Poems of 1839'

Anxious and worried while the white day goes dark,
I point my whip to the East, where the sky ends.
A fallen flower is not a bad thing,
From the spring mud, new flowers will rise.

己亥杂诗

龚自珍（清）

浩荡离愁白日斜，
吟鞭东指即天涯。
落红不是无情物，
化作春泥更护花。

BIOGRAPHIES

LUO BINWANG (640-684) together with Lu Zhaolin, Wang Bo, and Yang Jion, was considered one of the Four Paragons of the Early Tang. A child prodigy, he wrote "An Ode to the Geese" when he was seven years old.

LI QIAO (645-714) was a Tang Dynasty poet whose work was particularly admired for his 'youngwu shi', or 'poems on things'.

HE ZHIZHANG (659-744) was a statesman, but is remembered primarily as a poet. He is one of Du Fu's 'Eight Immortals of the Wine Cup', and famously gave Li Bai his by-name, "Banished Immortal" (zhexian).

Little is known about the Tang poet WANG ZHIHUAN (688-742), although the poem translated here, "Climbing White Stork Tower", is represented in the famous anthology, *Three Hundred Tang Poems,* edited in the 18th century.

MENG HAORAN was a contemporary of Li Bai, Wang Wei, and Du Fu, though he was older than the others. He had a brief career in government service, but lived most of his life in Hubei province, and wrote poems in celebration of a life of leisure. He was born around 689, and died in 740.

WANG HAN (687-726) was born into a wealthy family and was well known for his poems depicting life on the northern frontier. He held several government positions, and for a time, served as governor of Ruzhou. He had a reputation for being unrestrained and having a fondness for drink.

WANG CHANGLING (698-756), after passing the Imperial Examinations, held many official posts. He was one of the competitors in the famous wine shop competition, which also included the poets Wang Zhihuan and Gao Shi. He was killed in the An Lushan Rebellion.

WANG WEI (701-761) is one of the most famous and most accomplished poets in Chinese literature. He was a renowned calligrapher, musician, and politician, in addition to being one of his era's most beloved poets. Twenty-nine of his poems are included in *Three Hundred Tang Poems*.

LI BAI was one of China's greatest, and most beloved poets. A major poet of the Tang dynasty, he was born in 701, and died in 762. Though his poems often have a dream-like quality, Li celebrated nature and friendship, and quite frequently, the pleasures of drinking. An often-repeated story relates that while drunk, Li Bai reached into a river to embrace the moon and was drowned.

GAO SHI (C. 704-765) was honored with two poems that appeared in the anthology *Three Hundred Tang Poems*. He was born in poverty, but rose to become a secretary in the military and enjoyed a successful career in government. Along with Wang Zhihuan and Wang Changling, he was a competitor in the wine shop competition.

DU FU (712–770) is considered to be one of China's greatest poets, a label he frequently shares with his friend and fellow Tang poet Li Bai. His desire to be a civil servant was thwarted by the An Lushan Rebellion, and much of his life was spent in dire poverty. He is known for his great humanity, and his clear-eyed assessment of human nature.

Little is known about ZHANG JI (C. 712-779), except that he passed the Imperial Examinations, and worked for the Board of Revenue. The poem here is one of his few remaining poems, but it appears in *Three Hundred Tang Poems,* and is beloved in China. The Maple Bridge referred to in the poem is still standing.

MENG JIAO (751-814) was a Tang Dynasty poet who had two poems represented in *Three Hundred Tang Poems*. He spent many years as a recluse in southern China, and was associated with the Zen poet-monks there.

LIU ZONGYUAN (773-819) was a politician, poet, and founder of the so-called Classical Prose Movement. In addition to his poetry, he also produced fables, essays and travel writing.

ZHANG ZHIHE (730-c. 810) began his career as a public official, but was soon banished and became a wandering recluse. He loved to fish, though he famously used no bait, catching fish not being the goal. A Taoist by nature, he confounded his poet friends by refusing the comforts offered him, choosing to drift without a fixed address or abode.

LU LUN (739-799) was a poet whose life, like that of Du Fu, was disrupted by the An Lushan Rebellion. He is best known for having six poems represented in *Three Hundred Tang Poems.* Together with Li Yi, he is known for having revitalized the Frontier Fortress genre of Tang poetry.

LIU YUXI (772-842) grew up in the south, after his family was forced to move there following the An Lushan Rebellion. He held a number government positions, though he was periodically banished for writing political poems critical of the court. He was close to many other Tang poets, in particular Li Yi and Han Yu, who remained lifelong friends.

BAI JUYI (772-846), a poet well known to American readers as Po Chü-i, lived during the tumultuous period following the An Lushan Rebellion. Bai had a long career in government, serving as governor of Hangzhou and of Suzhou. He was instrumental in directing a number of water projects that helped local farmers, some of which still stand. Bai Juyi was prolific, leaving over 2,800 poems, which are still revered in China to this day.

Only four poems remain by the reclusive poet HU LINGNENG (785-826). Hu was from a poor family, and repaired pots and bowls for a living. He seems to have had no interest in an official career and lived as a hermit.

There is no record of LI SHEN's birth, but we know that he passed the Imperial Examinations, was briefly a professor, and later served as secretary to the war lord Li Qi. Li Shen was made governor of Shedong in 833, and served as chancellor under Emperor Wuzong. His poems often bemoaned the plight of poor farmers. Li Shen died in 846.

JIA DAO (779-843) spent time as a Buddhist monk before becoming a disciple of another Tang poet, Han Yu. Jia Dao failed several attempts to pass the official exams, and lived a life of poverty.

DU MU (803-852) was a leading poet of the late Tang Dynasty. He passed the Imperial Examinations in 828, and served in several minor government posts. He is known for his sensual lyrics, and for his *fu,* or poetic prose.

LI SHANGYIN (813-858) was a poet of the late Tang. Due to his political affiliations, Li never attained a high position in the government. He wrote in a variety of styles, though he is most famous for his untitled poems, which are of special interest to contemporary poets and critics in China.

LUO YIN (c. 833-910) took and failed the Imperial Examinations 10 times, and never held an official post until very late in life. His poems were well known and well-loved, but he could not translate that adoration into a successful life. He was known to be physically ugly, and of unpleasant disposition.

FAN ZHONGYAN (989-1052) was not only one of the leading poets of the Song Dynasty, he was a statesman, philosopher, and political leader who is considered one of the most important men in Chinese history. He was a principal member of the Neo-Confucianism movement, whose scholarly and philosophical works are considered to be on par with those of Confucius and Mencius. He was one of the most dominant personalities of the Song Dynasty.

WANG ANSHI (1021-1086) was a seminal character in the politics, governance, and poetry of the Song Dynasty. He served as chancellor, and attempted to initiate a series of political and economic reforms. Although successful at first, Wang fell out of favor with the emperor, and his reforms were rolled back. Wang's poetry has been compared to that of Du Fu, and his poetry and essays continue to be studied and read.

SU SHI, also referred to as Su Tung-po (1037-1101), was a preeminent poet of the Song Dynasty. In addition to his gifts as a poet, he was also a renowned calligrapher and painter. For most of his life, Su was a high-ranking government official, although he was twice exiled. After his final pardon, he retired from government work, began a period of Buddhist meditation, and produced many of his finest poems and paintings.

LI QINGZHAO (1084-1155) is generally regarded as China's greatest woman poet. Her father was a student of Su Shi, and while growing up she had access to a library of books and fine art. She and her husband, Zhao Mingchen, a scholar and government official with whom she enjoyed a loving marriage amassed a great collection of calligraphy and art, much of which was lost when their house was burned by the invading Jurchen army. Her husband died shortly after this event, and Li Qingzhao spent the rest of her life writing poetry and criticism.

LU YOU (1125-1210) was a prominent poet of the Southern Song Dynasty. He was extraordinarily prolific, writing more than 10,000 poems. He composed many powerfully patriotic poems, and was frequently demoted from his government position when he questioned the government's inability to take back the northern part of the country that had been conquered by invaders.

FAN CHENGDA (1126-1193) grew up in extreme poverty, but managed to pass the Imperial Examinations, and subsequently had a long and successful career in government. In addition to his poetry, he wrote important texts on geography and topology. His poems often show evidence of his youthful poverty and his interest in Buddhism. He was one of the most successful poets of the Song Dynasty.

YANG WANLI (1127-1206) was one of the 'Four Masters' of the Southern Song Dynasty. He passed the Imperial Examinations in 1154 and served in several minor official posts. Late in life he was exiled to Hangzhou, where he wrote poems celebrating the beauty of nature and the landscape around him.

ZHU XI (1130-1200) was one of the most influential Neo-Confucianist philosophers of the Song Dynasty, and many consider his teaching second only to Confucius himself. Zhu was also an acclaimed calligrapher, poet, and historian. He wrote almost 100 books and was an acclaimed scholar, but after attacks by a political rival, Zhu was executed. In 1228, Emperor Lizong honored him with the posthumous noble title, Duke of Hui.

Little is known about the Song poet LIN SHENG, though we know he wrote several poems condemning the rulers of the Southern Song Dynasty. He was buried in Xicheng Mountain, but his birth and death dates are a mystery.

YE SHAOWENG (1100-1151) was a poet of the Southern Song Dynasty connected with the Rivers and Lakes school of poetry. A Neo-Confucian, he was a historian and an academic, and his poetry is marked by direct, simple colloquialism.

Little is known about WENG JUAN, a poet of the Southern Song Dynasty, whose precise birth and death dates are a mystery. We do know that he failed to pass the Imperial Examinations, and spent his life in a remote mountain village. "April in the Countryside" is greatly admired in China, where it is represented in many anthologies and textbooks.

WANG MIAN (1287-1359) had intended to be a government official, but he found great acclaim as a poet, and especially as a painter. His paintings of plum blossoms in particular are revered as extraordinary, and a pinnacle of the art of the Yuan Dynasty. When Wang returned to his hometown after an itinerant life, he built his Plum Blossom Retreat, where he planted a thousand plum trees. One of his paintings graces the cover of this book.

YU QIAN (1398-1457), was a Ming Dynasty civil servant instrumental in protecting Beijing, the Ming capital, from Mongol invaders. Although his prowess in battle saved the city, he was later falsely accused of treason and executed. His identification with limestone in his poem in this collection is emblematic of his strong convictions.

ZHENG XIE (1693-1765) was a renowned painter and calligrapher who devoted himself to poetry later in life. His themes included ordinary people rendered in a colloquial idiom. He passed the Imperial Examinations in 1736 and served as a magistrate. His efforts on behalf of the poor met with resistance from wealthy power brokers, who forced him into exile.

YUAN MEI (1716-1798) passed his examinations at the early age of 23, and became a professor at Hanlin Academy. He served as a magistrate in several provinces before leaving public service to pursue a literary life. He had a keen interest in Chan (Zen) Buddhism, and is notable as a teacher for accepting female students, whom he often championed.

GAO DING (1828-1880) wrote compelling poems depicting landscape and nature, and is one of the few later poets whose work is included in the textbook for compulsory education in China. "Living in the Country" is his most famous poem.

GONG ZIZHEN (1792-1841) was the scion of a family of scholars and writers. He benefited from a classical education, and was steeped in literature and in the workings of government. He was greatly alarmed by the dangers of opium and the possible invasion by the British, but quit his official position when it became clear that he was powerless against these forces. He produced 27 volumes of poetry and hundreds of articles before his death at the age of 47.

THE TRANSLATORS

GARY YOUNG's most recent books are *That's What I Thought,* winner of the Lexi Rudnitsky Editor's Choice Award from Persea Books, and *Precious Mirror,* translations from the Japanese from White Pine Press. His books include *Even So: New and Selected Poems; Pleasure; No Other Life,* winner of the William Carlos Williams Award; *Braver Deeds,* winner of the Peregrine Smith Poetry Prize; *The Dream of a Moral Life* which won the James D. Phelan Award; and *Hands.* He has received a Pushcart Prize and grants from the National Endowment for the Humanities, National Endowment for the Arts, the California Arts Council, and the Vogelstein Foundation among others. In 2009 he received the Shelley Memorial Award from the Poetry Society of America. He teaches creative writing and directs the Cowell Press at the University of California, Santa Cruz.

YANWEN XU (徐研文) was born in Xuzhou, China. He is currently pursuing graduate studies in Computer Science at the University of California, Santa Cruz.

ACKNOWLEDGMENTS

Grateful acknowledgment is made to the following journals where many of these poems previously appeared:

The Bangalore Review: "April in the Countryside" by Weng Juan, "I Try to Enter a Garden but I Can't Get In" by Ye Shaoweng, "Writing on the Wall of an Inn in Lin'an" by Lin Sheng, "Spring Day" by Zhu Xi

Basalt: "I Walk Through My Gate Before Dawn to Feel the Cool Air" by Lu You, "Little Pool" by Yang Wanli, "At Dawn I Leave Jingci Temple to Bid Farewell to Lin Zifang" by Yang Wanli

Bear Review: "Gazing at Donting Lake" by Liu Yuxi, "The Countryside Is Lovely" by Du Fu

Better Than Starbucks: "A River in Spring for Hui Chong" by Su Shi, "Crossing the Border" by Wang Changling, "Bidding Farewell to Jian Xin Beside the Hibiscus Tower" by Wang Changling, "Docked by Maple Bridge at Night" by Zhang Ji, "Qingming Festival" by Du Mu

Cagibi: "April in the Countryside" by Weng Juan

Catamaran: "Gazing at Lu Shan Waterfall" by Li Bai

Chicago Quarterly Review: "Farewell to Yuaner Departing for Anxi" by Wang Wei, "On the Double Nine Festival, I think about my Brothers" by Wang Wei, "Fishermen on the River" by Fan Zhongyan

Cloudbank: "An Ode to the Willows" by He Zhizhang, "Spring Morning" by Meng Haoran

Gulf Coast: A Journal of Literature & Fine Arts: "At the Border" by Lu Lun, "Walking Alone by the Riverbank Looking for Flowers" by Du Fu

I-70 Review: "Spring in Jiangnan" by Du Mu, "A Pleasing Rain on a Spring Night" and "Quatrain (1)" by Du Fu, "Snow on the River" by Liu Zongyuan, "In Response to an Exam Question, I Write about 'Farewells on Ancient Ground'" by Bai Juyi

Mantis: "Farewell from Yellow Crane Tower to Meng Haoran Who Is Leaving for Yangzhou" by Li Bai, "Written on the Wall of Xi Lin Temple" by Su Shi, "A Four-line Poem Composed in Summer" by Li Qingzhao, "Gazing at Tianmen Mountain" by Li Bai, "Climbing White Stork Tower" by Wang Zhihuan

Miramar: "Written on Mr. Lake's Wall" by Wang Anshi, "Traveling Through the Mountains" by Du Mu, "Farewell to Dong Tinglan" by Gao Shi

Red Wheelbarrow: "Fisherman's Song" by Zhang Zhihe, "To My Son" by Lu You, "Traveler's Lament" by Meng Jiao, "On the Pond" by Bai Juyi, "June 27, I Write a Poem While Drunk in Wanghu Tower" by Su Shi, "Turning the Soil" by Li Shen, "Pity the Farmer" by Li Shen, "Walking in Moonlight" and "For Wan Lun" by Li Bai

SALT: "Night Thoughts" and "Departing Baidi City in Early Morning" by Li Bai

Spillway: "Wind" by Li Qiao, "A Song of Liangzhou" by Wang Zhihuan

Waxwing: "Seeking the Hidden One" by Jia Dao," "Waves of Sand" by Liu Yuxi

COMPANIONS FOR THE JOURNEY SERIES

Inspirational work by well-known writers in a small book format designed to
be carried along on your journey through life.

Volume 29
Taken to Heart
70 Poems from the Chinese
Translated by Gary Young and Yanwen Xu
978-1-945680-58-8 104 pages

Volume 28
Dreaming of Fallen Blossoms
Tune Poems of Su Dong-Po
Translated by Yun Wang
978-1-945680-27-4 243 pages

Volume 27
Precious Mirror
Kobun Otogawa
Translated by Gary Young
978-1-945680-21-1 100 pages

Volume 26
Unexpected Development
Klaus Merz
Translated by Marc Vincenz
978-1-945680-14-4 142 pages

Volume 25

A House by Itself

Selected Haiku: Masaoka Shiki

Translated by John Brandi & Noriko Kawasaki Martinez

ISBN 978-1-945680-09-0 102 pages

Volume 24

Poetics of Wonder: Passage to Mogdor

Alberto Ruy-Sánchez

Translated by Rhonda Dahl Buchanan

978-1-935210-55-9 156 pages

Volume 23

Searching for Guan Yin

Sarah E. Truman

978-1-935210-28-3 288 pages

Volume 22

Finding the Way Home

Poems of Awakening and Transformation

Edited by Dennis Maloney

978-1-935210-12-2 190 pages

Volume 21

What Happened Was . . .

On Writing Personal Essay and Memoir

Genie Zeiger

978-935210-04-7 106 pages

Volume 3
10,000 Dawns: The Love Poems of Claire and Yvan Goll
Translated by Thomas Rain Crowe and Nan Watkins
1-893996-27-1 88 pages

Volume 2
There Is No Road: Proverbs by Antonio Machado
Translated by Mary G. Berg and Dennis Maloney
1-893996-66-2 118 pages

Volume 1
Wild Ways: Zen Poems of Ikkyu
Translated by John Stevens
1-893996-65-4 152 pages